YOUR FIRST MILLION

THE PRACTICAL PATH FROM BROKE TO BREAKTHROUGH

DESHAWN PRICE

HERITAGE
PUBLISHING

This book is dedicated to the builders who got tired of almost, tired of someday, and tired of "it could have been." To the ones who decided that excuses had run out and execution would take their place. To those who worked in obscurity, improved in silence, and kept producing when applause was nowhere to be found.

To the disciplined few who chose skill over shortcuts, ownership over comfort, and cash flow over image. To the men and women who turned late nights into launch pads and small wins into scaling systems. To those who refused to let a broke season become a broke identity.

To the risk-takers who moved before they felt ready, the learners who applied instead of admired, and the executors who finished what they started. To every person who chose construction over consumption and production over procrastination.

If you are willing to build when it's boring, persist when it's slow, and execute when it's hard — this path is yours.

Now go earn the story this dedication was written for.

"Execution is the bridge between intention and income.

Ownership is the bridge between effort and freedom.

Discipline is the bridge between where you are and what you are worth.

Build the bridge — then walk it daily."

FOREWORD

Most people say they want financial freedom. Far fewer are willing to live the days that create it. They want the breakthrough, but resist the build. They want the outcome, but avoid the output. They admire results, but negotiate with discipline. This book does not exist to motivate spectators — it exists to activate builders.

You are about to read a manual for economic responsibility and personal execution. Not theory-heavy optimism. Not inspirational fluff. Not lottery thinking dressed in business language. What follows is a practical, demanding path that puts results on the other side of repeated action. It will challenge your habits, confront your comfort, and expose the hidden costs of delay. Good. That is exactly what a breakthrough requires.

The principles in these pages are not complicated — but they are not optional. Produce before you polish. Execute before you feel ready. Stack skills. Protect cash flow. Multiply value. Eliminate excuses. Repeat without drama. Wealth is rarely blocked by lack of information. It is blocked by lack of sustained implementation.

If you read this casually, nothing will change. If you apply this aggressively, everything can.

Do not look for permission in these pages — look for instruction. Do not look for hype — look for handles you can grab and use immediately. The line between broke and breakthrough is narrower than most think, but it is crossed by action, not agreement.

Read with a pen. Decide quickly. Execute immediately. Build relentlessly.

Your move starts now.

INTRODUCTION

Most people don't fail to reach a million dollars because they lack opportunity — they fail because they never adopt a millionaire standard of thinking, discipline, and execution. This book is not here to comfort you. It is here to confront you. If you are looking for shortcuts, secret tricks, or lottery-ticket fantasies, you're in the wrong place. Wealth is not built on wishes. It is built on decisions made daily, consistently, and often painfully.

Being broke is not just a financial condition — it is a behavioral pattern. It shows up in delayed action, scattered focus, comfort addiction, and unmanaged risk. The breakthrough you want will demand a different version of you than the one who started this journey. More focused. More decisive. More accountable. This path will ask you to measure your habits, not your intentions. Intentions never built a fortune. Systems do.

Your first million is not about money first — it is about value creation, ownership, leverage, and disciplined repetition. You will learn to think in assets instead of hours, outcomes instead of activity, and multiplication instead of maintenance. You will be challenged to eliminate low-yield behaviors and replace them with high-impact moves. Not someday — now.

There will be moments where quitting will feel reasonable. That is exactly where most people stop — and exactly where uncommon earners push forward. The separating line between broke and breakthrough is rarely intelligence. It is endurance with direction.

This book will push you to audit your time, your circle, your skills, your spending, and your excuses. It will challenge your definitions of security and risk. It will require you to stop waiting for permission and start building with what you already have.

No hype. No fluff. No rescue coming.

Only a practical path — and your decision to walk it.

PREFACE

This book was not written for the curious — it was written for the committed. It is for the reader who is finished with financial drift and ready for deliberate construction. If you are looking for easy promises, fast fantasies, or feel-good theories about money, you will find friction here instead. That friction is intentional. Breakthrough is not born from comfort reading but from confronting patterns that no longer serve you.

The path to your first million is not hidden, but it is often ignored. It is built on production, ownership, skill stacking, cash flow discipline, and relentless execution. None of these are mysterious. All of them are demanding. Most people fail financially not because they lack access to knowledge, but because they lack sustained applied action. Knowledge that is not executed becomes decoration. Execution that is repeated becomes transformation.

These pages are designed to be practical and confrontational by design. You will be challenged to audit your schedule, your habits, your standards, your excuses, and your output. Not to create guilt — but to create leverage. Clarity is leverage. Measurement is leverage. Ownership is leverage. When you see clearly, you can act precisely. When you act precisely, progress accelerates.

You do not need perfect conditions to begin. You need honest evaluation and immediate movement. Start small, but start real. Build one offer. Create one asset. Improve one skill. Ship one project. Then repeat without waiting for applause.

This preface is your line in the sand. Read forward only if you are willing to execute.

1

YOUR EXCUSES ARE EXPENSIVE — AND YOU'RE PAYING DAILY

Your excuses are not harmless thoughts drifting through your mind — they are daily financial withdrawals from your future account. Every delay, every rationalization, every soft promise to start tomorrow is a silent transaction against your potential. You may not see the charge immediately, but the compounding effect is brutal over time. Excuses feel emotionally cheap in the moment because they buy relief from discomfort. That relief, however, is purchased with forfeited growth. The marketplace rewards motion, not intention. Comfort gives you emotional candy while stealing your long-term strength. Every time you choose avoidance over action, you reinforce a broke pattern of behavior. Patterns become habits, and habits become outcomes. Outcomes eventually become your lifestyle whether you planned them or not.

Most people think poverty begins in the wallet, but it actually begins in the decision loop. The habit of post-poning hard things creates financial fragility long before bills pile up. When you repeatedly delay skill-building, risk-taking, and disciplined work, you train yourself to hesitate at opportunity. Hesitation is expensive because speed matters in value creation. The person who acts imperfectly learns faster than the person who plans perfectly. Learning speed is income speed. Income speed compounds into wealth capacity. Wealth capacity expands into ownership and leverage. All of that is slowed down by the reflex to excuse delay. You don't need a new personality to earn more — you need a new response time. The faster you obey your highest priority task, the cheaper your future becomes.

Excuses often disguise themselves as intelligence and caution. You tell yourself you are being strategic when you are actually being avoidant. You say you are researching when you are really hiding. Preparation has a finish line, but excuses never do. They keep moving the starting gate farther away. The mind can generate endless reasons why now is not ideal. Ideal conditions are the favorite fiction of the stagnant. Momentum is built in motion, not in theory. Action clarifies faster than analysis. The wealthy learn by doing and adjusting, not by waiting and wondering. Your bank account grows at the speed of executed decisions.

You are paying daily through distraction taxes. Every hour lost to low-value consumption is an hour not invested in skill or asset creation. Entertainment is not evil, but unmanaged entertainment is expensive. Your attention is your most valuable currency before money ever is. Where attention goes, capability grows. Where capability grows, income follows. If your attention is scattered, your earning power will be scattered. Focus is a financial strategy, not just a productivity trick. Guarded attention produces concentrated value. Concentrated value produces market demand. Market demand produces income opportunity.

Another hidden cost of excuses is identity erosion. Each broken promise to yourself weakens your internal authority. When you no longer believe your own commitments, discipline collapses. Without discipline, consistency dies. Without consistency, compounding cannot start. Compounding is the engine of the first million. Small daily actions, repeated without drama, create disproportionate outcomes. Excuses interrupt repetition. Interrupted repetition kills compounding. You do not need heroic bursts — you need stubborn continuity. The person who trusts their own word moves faster and risks smarter. Self-trust is an underrated wealth asset.

Social excuses are equally expensive. Blaming your environment feels relieving but produces zero leverage. You cannot monetize blame. You cannot invest resentment. You cannot scale victimhood. Ownership thinking is profitable thinking. When you take responsibility, you gain control variables. Control variables allow experimentation. Experimentation produces data. Data produces improvement. Improvement produces income expansion. The moment you say, "It's on me," your options multiply. Power always follows responsibility.

Time-based excuses are especially dangerous because they sound responsible. You claim you will start when life slows down. Life rarely slows down on its own. Priority is not found — it is assigned. The calendar reveals truth faster than your intentions do. If wealth-building tasks are not scheduled, they are fictional. Scheduled work becomes real work. Real work produces measurable output. Measurable output can be improved. Improvement increases yield. Yield accelerates progress. Progress builds motivation. Motivation then reinforces discipline.

Emotional excuses create another layer of cost. You wait to feel confident before acting. Confidence is usually the result of action, not the prerequisite. Action generates evidence. Evidence builds belief. Belief strengthens confidence. Waiting reverses the order and stalls the engine. Professionals act with incomplete emotion all the time. They do not negotiate with mood — they execute commitments. Your feelings are real but not reliable drivers of financial progress. Systems outperform emotions every time. Install systems and your feelings will eventually follow your results.

Financial excuses themselves can become circular traps. You say you cannot start because you lack money. Many wealth paths begin with skill and service, not capital. Skills can be built with time and repetition. Service can be offered with effort and reliability. Reliability builds reputation. Reputation attracts opportunity. Opportunity produces revenue. Revenue can be reinvested. Reinvestment builds assets. Assets generate cash flow. Cash flow builds freedom. The circle starts with usefulness, not funding.

Comparison excuses are motivation poison. Watching others succeed can either instruct you or paralyze you. If you use comparison as proof that you are behind, you will stall. If you use it as proof that success is possible, you will move. Someone else's chapter ten should not cancel your chapter one. Progress is personal but principles are universal. Skill stacking works for anyone who applies it. Market value rises for anyone who solves real problems. Discipline pays anyone who practices it. Ownership rewards anyone who pursues it. The gate is not locked — it is crowded with quitters. Stay longer than they do.

Perfection excuses are elite-level procrastination. You refine plans endlessly to avoid imperfect exposure. The market does not reward perfect drafts — it rewards delivered value. Version one in the marketplace beats version ten in your head. Feedback requires exposure. Exposure requires courage. Courage grows through use. Use creates experience. Experience produces judgment. Judgment improves decisions. Better decisions increase returns. Returns finance better tools. Better tools increase scale.

Energy excuses also drain wealth potential. You say you are too tired to build more. Fatigue is often mismanaged focus, not absolute depletion. Low-value work drains more than high-value work energizes. When you work on meaningful creation, energy often rises. Physical health supports financial endurance. Sleep, movement, and nutrition are income multipliers. A weak body struggles to hold strong discipline. A strong routine supports sustained output. Sustained output produces compounding progress. Compounding progress reduces long-term strain. Strength is practical, not optional.

Network excuses limit exposure to opportunity. You claim you do not know the right people. Value attracts valuable relationships over time. Start by becoming useful, not connected. Contribution opens doors faster than credentials. People remember problem-solvers. Problem-solvers get invited back. Repeated invitations build networks. Networks create deal flow. Deal flow creates options. Options create leverage. Leverage accelerates wealth. Generosity is often a gateway to access.

Fear-based excuses pretend to be protection. They promise safety but deliver stagnation. Risk cannot be eliminated, only managed. Small calculated risks teach faster than safe inactivity. Each managed risk expands your competence boundary. Expanded competence reduces future risk. The safest long-term position is adaptability.

Adaptability grows through trial. Trial requires exposure. Exposure feels uncomfortable but pays educational dividends. Education applied becomes income. Income diversified becomes stability.

Habit excuses hide in language. You say "that's just how I am" as if behavior were fixed. Identity is more flexible than you think. Repeated action reshapes self-image. Self-image reshapes choices. Choices reshape outcomes. Outcomes reinforce identity again. Change the loop at the action level. Small behavior shifts create identity drift. Identity drift creates lifestyle change. Lifestyle change creates financial difference. You are more editable than your excuses claim. Edit aggressively.

Technology excuses are modern but weak. Tools are more available than ever before. Distribution is cheaper than ever before. Learning is more accessible than ever before. Gatekeepers are fewer than ever before. The barrier now is discipline, not access. Execution beats access every time. Tools unused are worthless. Tools applied are transformative. Digital leverage favors the consistent. Consistency beats brilliance in open markets. Show up and ship.

Your first million is less about brilliance and more about excuse elimination. Remove delay and output rises. Remove distraction and focus rises. Remove blame and control rises. Remove perfectionism and speed rises. Remove fear and experimentation rises. Remove comparison and confidence rises. Remove comfort addiction and discipline rises. Each removed excuse is a revenue upgrade. Each disciplined action is a deposit. Deposits compound into capacity. Capacity compounds into wealth.

The daily payment plan of excuses is optional. You can cancel it starting today. Replace each excuse with a micro-action. Replace each delay with a scheduled step. Replace each fear with a small test. Replace each doubt with a measurable attempt. Replace each complaint with a correction. Replace each distraction with a boundary. Replace each intention with execution. Replace each story with data. Replace each someday with today. Your future balance sheet is waiting for different behavior.

2

BROKE IS NOT A BANK BALANCE — IT'S A THINKING PATTERN

Broke is not first a number in your bank account — it is a pattern in your thinking that repeats itself through your decisions. A low balance is often just the visible symptom of invisible habits. The marketplace rarely withholds money from disciplined value creators for long. When income stays low year after year, the cause is usually behavioral, not circumstantial. Thinking patterns drive daily choices, and daily choices drive financial direction. If your default response is delay, distraction, and dependence, your finances will mirror it. If your default response becomes ownership, initiative, and execution, your finances will eventually reflect that too. Money follows mental frameworks more than motivational bursts. A person can receive a windfall and stay broke in mindset. That mindset will spend, avoid, and excuse its way back to zero. Until the thinking changes, the numbers cannot stay changed.

A broke thinking pattern prioritizes comfort over capacity building. It chooses easy consumption over difficult creation. It seeks relief today instead of strength tomorrow. It spends emotional energy avoiding effort instead of applying effort. It negotiates with discipline instead of installing discipline. It treats learning as optional instead of essential. It looks for hacks instead of habits. It wants results without repetition. It values appearance over ability. That pattern guarantees financial fragility regardless of starting point.

Broke thinking also measures effort emotionally instead of economically. It says, "I tried," instead of asking, "Did it produce?" The market does not reward sincerity alone — it rewards solved problems. Output matters more than intention. Measurable value beats visible busyness. Activity is not automatically progress. Many people stay tired but unproductive because they confuse motion with leverage. Leverage multiplies results without multiplying hours. Broke thinking resists leverage because leverage requires learning and systems. Systems feel harder at first but easier forever after.

Another sign of broke thinking is dependency on permission. Waiting to be chosen keeps you from choosing yourself. Waiting to be hired keeps you from building capability. Waiting to be discovered keeps you from becoming discoverable. Ownership thinking creates projects instead of waiting for positions. It builds platforms instead of begging for platforms. It publishes, produces, and prototypes. It does not wait for applause before effort. It does not require consensus before starting. It moves with conviction and adjusts with feedback. Permissionless progress is a wealth accelerator.

Broke thinking treats time as something to spend instead of something to invest. Hours disappear into low-return routines. Evenings dissolve into passive consumption. Weekends become recovery from unfocused weeks. Investment thinking assigns time to asset-building actions. Skills are practiced deliberately. Relationships are cultivated intentionally. Projects are advanced measurably. Recovery is structured, not accidental. Energy is managed like capital. Attention is budgeted like money. Time becomes a portfolio, not a landfill.

Scarcity language reinforces broke thinking. Saying "I can't afford that" often ends the thought process too early. A stronger question is "How could I afford that?" The first closes doors while the second opens strategies. Questions shape creativity. Creative thinking produces options. Options create paths. Paths enable progress. Progress builds confidence. Confidence encourages bigger attempts. Bigger attempts create bigger returns. Language programs behavior quietly but powerfully. Upgrade the questions and you upgrade the outcomes.

Broke thinking avoids numbers and measurement. It operates on feelings and guesses. Wealth thinking tracks metrics and adjusts behavior. What gets measured gets improved. Revenue, conversion, hours of deep work, skill reps — these are controllable variables. Control creates confidence. Confidence increases pace. Pace increases opportunity surface area. More opportunities produce more wins. Measurement turns effort into data. Data turns hope into strategy. Strategy turns motion into momentum.

Another pattern is short-term emotional spending. Purchases become mood regulation tools. Stress triggers buying instead of building. Celebration triggers splurging instead of scaling. Relief triggers escape instead of evaluation. This cycle prevents capital formation. Capital is required for ownership moves. Ownership moves create wealth inflection points. Broke thinking consumes seed instead of planting it. Wealth thinking protects seed capital fiercely. It understands that small reserves create big options. Options are financial oxygen.

Broke thinking fears skill difficulty. It avoids steep learning curves. It chooses familiar weakness over unfamiliar growth. High-income skills often feel uncomfortable at first. Selling, negotiating, building, leading — these stretch identity. Stretching feels risky but pays dividends. Avoiding stretch feels safe but costs opportunity. Skill acquisition is one of the highest-return investments available. Skills cannot be repossessed. Skills travel across industries. Skills stack into uniqueness. Unique value commands premium pay.

Blame is another anchor of broke thinking. Externalizing every setback prevents internal upgrades. When everything is someone else's fault, nothing becomes your responsibility to fix. Responsibility is power disguised as pressure. Owning the problem gives you authority over the solution. Authority enables action. Action enables correction. Correction improves results. Results build momentum. Momentum attracts resources. Resources expand reach. Reach increases income potential.

Broke thinking resists delayed gratification. It wants visible reward immediately. Wealth often grows invisibly before it shows publicly. The early phases are quiet and repetitive. Savings build slowly. Skills sharpen privately. Networks grow gradually. Systems improve incrementally. The harvest comes after the planting season. Those who quit early never see the yield. Patience is not passive — it is disciplined consistency. Consistency compounds into advantage. Advantage produces asymmetrical returns.

Environment selection also reveals thinking patterns.

Broke thinking stays in circles that normalize stagnation. It tolerates conversations that kill ambition. It accepts peer pressure toward mediocrity. Wealth thinking upgrades rooms intentionally. It seeks proximity to builders. It studies performers. It listens to producers. Conversations shift toward solutions. Standards rise through exposure. Expectation levels climb. Behavior adjusts upward. Environment is a silent strategist.

Broke thinking confuses security with sameness. It clings to routines that no longer produce growth. It fears calculated change. Wealth thinking defines security as adaptability. It builds multiple skills, multiple channels, multiple options. Diversification begins with capability, not capital. Capability diversification reduces risk. Reduced risk allows bolder moves. Bolder moves create bigger upside. Upside funds resilience. Resilience supports longevity. Longevity increases probability of success.

Consumption without creation is another pattern trap. Endless learning without application becomes intellectual entertainment. Courses watched but not implemented have zero return. Notes taken but not executed produce no income. Creation turns knowledge into value. Value attracts compensation. Compensation funds reinvestment. Reinvestment increases scale. Scale multiplies results. Results reinforce discipline. Discipline sustains creation. Creation breaks the broke cycle.

Broke thinking is reactive instead of proactive. It responds to bills instead of building buffers. It responds to crises instead of designing prevention. Proactive planning reduces volatility. Reduced volatility preserves capital. Preserved capital enables opportunity moves. Opportunity moves create growth. Growth creates margin. Margin creates peace. Peace supports better decisions. Better decisions increase yield. The cycle flips from survival to strategy.

Identity again sits at the center of the pattern. If you see yourself as perpetually behind, you will act cautiously and inconsistently. If you see yourself as a builder in progress, you will act constructively and persistently. Identity drives tolerance for effort. Builders tolerate repetition. Builders expect obstacles. Builders measure progress in iterations. Iterations produce improvement. Improvement produces confidence. Confidence increases scope. Scope increases reward. Self-concept is a financial lever.

Broke thinking treats failure as verdict instead of feedback. One loss becomes a stopping point. Wealth thinking treats failure as data. Data informs adjustment. Adjustment improves probability. Improved probability encourages re-entry. Re-entry produces wins. Wins build resilience. Resilience supports bigger plays. Bigger plays produce bigger outcomes. Outcomes justify endurance. Endurance separates earners from quitters.

Gratitude and ambition are not opposites in wealth thinking. You can appreciate what you have while building what you want. Broke thinking uses contentment as a shield against effort. Wealth thinking uses gratitude as fuel for stewardship. Stewardship multiplies resources. Multiplication increases responsibility. Responsibility increases discipline. Discipline increases capacity. Capacity increases contribution. Contribution increases compensation. The cycle becomes generative, not stagnant.

The shift from broke to breakthrough begins in thought patterns before it appears in bank statements. Upgrade the pattern and behavior follows. Upgrade behavior and results follow. Upgrade results and identity follows. The process is reversible and repeatable. No one is locked into a permanent pattern. Mental models can be rebuilt deliberately. Questions can be upgraded intentionally. Habits can be trained progressively. Discipline can be strengthened daily. Your thinking pattern is not your prison — it is your starting point for change.

3

COMFORT IS THE SILENT KILLER OF WEALTH

Comfort is rarely loud, rarely dramatic, and rarely questioned, yet it quietly dismantles more financial futures than failure ever does. It wraps itself in reason, routine, and relaxation until stagnation feels justified. You don't wake up one day destroyed by comfort — you drift there gradually. The chair gets softer, the standards get lower, and the urgency fades. Comfort convinces you that maintenance is progress. It teaches you to protect ease instead of expanding capacity. Wealth, however, is built in the stretch zone, not the safe zone. Growth requires friction, and friction is uncomfortable by design. The moment your life has zero productive tension, your earning curve starts flattening. Comfort never announces the damage while it is happening.

Comfort trains you to avoid necessary difficulty. It persuades you to choose familiar tasks over profitable ones. You answer easy emails instead of making hard sales calls. You organize files instead of building offers. You tweak logos instead of testing products. You research endlessly instead of releasing version one. These substitutions feel productive but produce little leverage. Low-discomfort work usually has low economic value. High-value work usually carries emotional resistance. If you always choose the path of least discomfort, you choose the path of least income. The pattern is predictable and costly.

The danger of comfort is that it feels earned. After small wins, you feel entitled to coast. After progress, you feel justified to pause too long. Recovery turns into residence. Breaks become lifestyles. The hunger that built momentum gets replaced with maintenance thinking. Maintenance thinking preserves — it does not multiply. Wealth requires multiplication strategies. Multiplication requires motion and experimentation. Experimentation requires risk and exposure. Exposure feels uncomfortable but pays educational dividends. Comfort blocks the very conditions that create scaling.

Comfort also distorts risk perception. It makes small risks feel huge and huge risks feel invisible. Sending a proposal feels terrifying while staying underpaid feels acceptable. Launching a service feels scary while wasting years feels normal. This inversion keeps people financially stuck. The real risk is long-term underperformance. The real danger is unused potential. The real cost is delayed ownership. Short-term discomfort often prevents long-term hardship. Long-term comfort often creates long-term limitation. You must retrain your risk lens. Measure danger in decades, not days.

Routine comfort can become an income ceiling. When your schedule is built entirely around convenience, it cannot support expansion. Expansion requires added effort before added reward. Early mornings, late drafts, extra reps — these stretch capacity. Capacity is the container for higher income. A small container cannot hold large returns.

Most people try to increase income without increasing capacity. That mismatch causes stress and collapse. Increase your workload tolerance strategically. Increase your focus endurance deliberately. Build a bigger container before demanding bigger inflow.

Comfort seeks entertainment over education. It defaults to passive consumption. It chooses scrolling over studying. It prefers watching builders instead of becoming one. This creates admiration without acquisition. You feel inspired but unchanged. Inspiration without implementation is emotional sugar. It tastes good but builds nothing. Skill comes from drills, not documentaries. Mastery comes from reps, not reels. Wealth follows mastery far more than motivation. Replace some entertainment with execution and your trajectory shifts.

Financial comfort at a low level is especially dangerous. When your bills are barely covered, you feel stable enough not to push. This is the plateau trap. Urgency disappears before abundance arrives. You stop climbing because you are no longer desperate. Desperation leaving is good, but discipline must replace it. Without discipline, progress stalls. Stalled progress erodes optionality. Optionality is critical to wealth building. Multiple options reduce dependence. Reduced dependence increases negotiation power. Negotiation power increases income. Do not confuse survival stability with success.

Comfort hides inside social approval. It encourages you to fit in instead of stand out. Standing out invites judgment. Judgment feels uncomfortable. Yet premium value often comes from differentiated effort. Extra preparation looks excessive to average performers. Deep focus looks antisocial to distracted groups. Ambition looks arrogant to the uncommitted. If you obey comfort-driven social norms, you cap your ceiling. High performers tolerate misunderstanding. They trade approval for advancement. Advancement compounds into authority and income.

Physical comfort affects financial endurance more than most admit. Sedentary habits weaken energy and clarity. Low energy reduces output quality. Reduced output reduces opportunity capture. Movement sharpens cognition. Strength supports stamina. Stamina supports consistency. Consistency supports compounding. Compounding builds wealth. Care for your body as an economic asset. Train it to support long execution cycles. Energy is revenue potential in biological form.

Comfort also resists measurement and accountability. It prefers vague effort over tracked performance. Numbers create pressure. Pressure creates discomfort. Discomfort creates growth signals. When you track output, you confront truth. Truth forces adjustment. Adjustment improves yield. Yield motivates repetition. Repetition builds momentum. Momentum builds confidence. Confidence supports bigger targets. Targets stretch behavior upward.

The comfort of anonymity keeps many from publishing, selling, and promoting. Visibility feels risky. Exposure invites feedback. Feedback can sting. Yet invisibility guarantees low opportunity flow. Opportunity flows toward visible value. Publish your ideas. Share your solutions. Offer your services. Make your work findable. Marketing is service at scale. Scale multiplies income potential. Hide less and help more. The market cannot reward what it cannot see.

Comfort prefers certainty over possibility. It wants guaranteed outcomes before committed effort. Guarantees are rare in entrepreneurship and ownership. Probability improves through preparation, not hesitation. You build odds in your favor through reps. Reps require starting before certainty. Early uncertainty is the tuition of mastery. Pay it willingly. Tuition produces capability. Capability produces confidence. Confidence enables bolder plays. Bold plays produce asymmetric upside. Upside builds wealth inflection points.

Relationship comfort can also limit growth. Keeping only easy relationships shrinks perspective. Growth relationships challenge assumptions. They ask harder questions. They expect higher standards. Standards feel uncomfortable but elevate performance. Performance attracts opportunity. Opportunity expands income channels. Channels diversify revenue. Diversified revenue stabilizes progress. Stability allows strategic risk. Strategic risk fuels expansion.

Comfort delays difficult conversations about money. Avoiding pricing talks, negotiation, and boundaries keeps income low. Clear value deserves clear pricing. Pricing confidence requires self-respect. Self-respect grows through competence. Competence grows through practice. Practice requires exposure. Exposure feels uncomfortable but increases skill. Skill increases earning power. Earning power increases choice. Choice increases freedom. Freedom is funded by courageous conversations.

Creative comfort keeps ideas in notebooks instead of markets. Private perfection feels safer than public iteration. But private ideas earn nothing. Public prototypes produce feedback. Feedback produces refinement. Refinement produces product-market fit. Fit produces revenue. Revenue funds improvement. Improvement increases scale. Scale increases reach. Reach increases return. Ship before you feel fully ready.

Comfort is addictive because it removes strain signals. Strain signals are growth indicators. When muscles strain, they strengthen. When skills strain, they sharpen. When courage strains, it expands. Remove all strain and you remove adaptation. No adaptation means no improvement. No improvement means no advantage. No advantage means average returns. Average returns rarely create millions. Productive strain is a wealth ally. Learn to welcome it.

You must schedule discomfort deliberately. Do one hard revenue-producing task early each day. Make the difficult call first. Build the complex piece first. Solve the high-value problem first. Early wins create momentum. Momentum reduces resistance. Reduced resistance increases pace. Increased pace increases attempts. More attempts increase wins. Wins reinforce discipline. Discipline sustains growth.

Comfort will always offer a reasonable alternative to bold action. It will suggest tomorrow, later, after, eventually. Those words are expensive. Replace them with now, next, done, shipped. Action vocabulary creates action behavior. Behavior creates measurable output. Output creates opportunity. Opportunity creates income. Income creates reinvestment. Reinvestment creates scale. Scale creates wealth. Vocabulary shapes velocity.

Wealth builders build a tolerance for constructive discomfort. They treat discomfort like a training partner. It signals where growth lives. It marks the edge of expansion. Step into it repeatedly and it shrinks. Avoid it repeatedly and it grows. Your comfort zone should be visited, not lived in. Rest there briefly, then leave again. Recovery is strategic — residence is destructive. Visit comfort, don't build a house there.

4

STOP CONSUMING — START CONSTRUCTING INCOME

Consumption is the default mode of the distracted, but construction is the discipline of the wealthy. If you do not deliberately choose to build, you will automatically drift into buying, watching, scrolling, and absorbing. Modern systems are engineered to keep you consuming because consumers are predictable and profitable. Builders, however, are independent and disruptive. Every hour you spend only taking in information without producing value keeps you financially stationary. Consumption feels active but often creates no assets. Construction feels harder but produces leverage. Leverage is what turns effort into multiplication. Multiplication is what turns income into wealth. The shift from consumer to constructor is the turning point of your financial life. Until you make that shift, progress will remain slow and fragile.

You cannot consume your way to your first million. More books, more podcasts, more videos, and more courses will not save you if they do not convert into output. Information without implementation is intellectual clutter. It feels productive but produces no return. The marketplace does not pay you for what you know — it pays you for what you deploy. Deployment requires risk and visibility. Visibility requires courage and repetition. Repetition creates competence. Competence creates confidence. Confidence accelerates contribution. Contribution attracts compensation.

Most people over-invest in learning and under-invest in building. They prepare endlessly but release nothing. They outline businesses they never start. They design brands they never launch. They study markets they never enter. This is construction avoidance disguised as preparation. Preparation has a purpose — to enable action. When preparation replaces action, it becomes procrastination. Action creates feedback. Feedback creates improvement. Improvement creates income. Income funds expansion.

Construction begins with creating value that did not exist before your effort. That value can be a service, a product, a system, or a solution. It can be digital or physical. It can be simple or complex. What matters is usefulness. Usefulness is monetizable. The more specific the usefulness, the higher the value. General effort produces general pay. Specific solutions produce premium pay. Look for problems and build answers. Answers are assets in motion.

Your daily schedule reveals whether you are consuming or constructing. Constructors allocate prime hours to output. Consumers allocate prime hours to input. Constructors create before they browse. Consumers browse before they begin. Constructors ship imperfect work. Consumers polish private drafts forever. Constructors measure deliverables. Consumers measure intentions. Constructors build pipelines. Consumers build playlists. The difference compounds financially.

Digital consumption is the most deceptive trap. It feels like engagement while draining creative energy. Endless scrolling fractures attention. Fractured attention weakens execution. Weak execution reduces results. Reduced results kill motivation. Low motivation increases passive behavior. Passive behavior increases consumption. The loop feeds itself. You must interrupt it deliberately. Set boundaries on intake. Protect blocks for creation. Creation restores agency.

Income construction requires producing things that work without your constant presence. That means assets and systems. Assets include content, products, tools, and intellectual property. Systems include processes that deliver value repeatedly. Repeated delivery creates recurring revenue. Recurring revenue builds stability. Stability allows reinvestment. Reinvestment accelerates growth. Growth increases options. Options increase leverage. Leverage multiplies income.

Start constructing with what you know and where you are. You do not need perfect conditions. You need applied usefulness. Teach what you understand. Build what you can solve. Improve what is broken around you. Document what you learn. Package what you practice. Offer what you test. Iterate what you ship. Each cycle increases value. Each version improves market fit.

Consumption seeks entertainment first and effort second. Construction reverses that order. Work comes before reward. Output comes before applause. Contribution comes before compensation. This sequence feels unfair to consumers but natural to builders. Builders understand delayed gratification. They invest effort upfront. They harvest returns later. That delay is the gateway to scale. Scale never appears instantly.

You must replace passive habits with productive rituals. Instead of watching another tutorial, apply one lesson. Instead of reading another book, build one project. Instead of planning another idea, test one offer. Replace intake with iteration. Replace theory with trials. Replace notes with prototypes. Replace saving with shipping. Replace browsing with building. Rituals determine results.

Construction also means constructing skills, not just products. Skills are portable assets. They generate income across contexts. High-value skills include selling, writing, building, analyzing, and leading. Skill construction requires drills. Drills require repetition. Repetition requires discipline. Discipline requires scheduling. Scheduling requires priority. Priority requires decision. Decision requires commitment. Commitment produces mastery.

Consumers seek discounts while constructors seek margins. Consumers ask how cheap. Constructors ask how valuable. Value thinking creates premium positioning. Premium positioning increases revenue per effort unit. Higher revenue per unit accelerates wealth building. Low-margin thinking requires endless volume. Endless volume creates burnout. Margin thinking creates sustainability. Sustainability supports longevity. Longevity supports compounding. Compounding builds millions.

Construction demands public accountability. When you publish work, you commit to standards. Standards raise performance. Performance attracts trust. Trust attracts buyers. Buyers create revenue. Revenue funds improvement. Improvement raises standards again. The cycle strengthens your market presence. Private consumption produces none of this. Private learning is invisible. Invisible work rarely earns. Visible value does.

Stop measuring progress by what you finish reading and start measuring by what you finish releasing. Releases create opportunity surface area. More releases mean more chances for wins. More wins mean more capital. More capital means more reinvestment. More reinvestment means more scale. Scale increases reach. Reach increases revenue potential. Revenue potential increases motivation. Motivation fuels continued construction.

Construction is uncomfortable because it exposes your current limits. That exposure is educational. Education through action is sticky. You remember what you build. You forget what you browse. Built knowledge becomes operational. Operational knowledge becomes profitable. Profitable knowledge becomes scalable. Scalable knowledge becomes wealth-producing. Wealth-producing systems become freedom engines. Freedom is constructed, not consumed. No one binge-watches their way to independence.

Replace the question "What should I watch next?" with "What should I build next?" That one shift rewires behavior. Behavior change rewires identity. Identity change rewires outcomes. Outcomes change lifestyle. Lifestyle changes legacy. Legacy is built through creation. Creation requires courage. Courage requires action. Action requires decision. Decide to construct.

Your first million will not come from being the best-informed spectator. It will come from being a relentless builder. Build offers. Build skills. Build systems. Build assets. Build networks. Build discipline. Build output volume. Build feedback loops. Build value repeatedly. Construction is the practical path from broke to breakthrough.

5

YOUR FIRST DOLLAR OF OWNERSHIP CHANGES EVERYTHING

Your first dollar of ownership is more powerful than your next thousand dollars of wages. Wages pay you once, but ownership can pay you repeatedly. The moment you earn from something you control, your financial identity begins to shift. You stop being only a participant and start becoming a producer. That shift is psychological before it is mathematical. It changes how you evaluate time, effort, and opportunity. You begin to ask different questions about leverage and scale. You look for systems instead of shifts. You measure assets instead of hours. One owned dollar teaches more than a thousand observed ones. Ownership rewires ambition.

Employment income depends on permission and continuation. Ownership income depends on value and demand. Permission-based money can be paused by others. Value-based money can be multiplied by you. When you own even a tiny asset, you experience asymmetric reward. Your effort is no longer locked to a clock. The result can exceed the hour. That possibility expands your thinking. Expanded thinking creates new experiments. Experiments produce discovery. Discovery produces opportunity. Opportunity produces acceleration.

The first ownership dollar proves that independence is not theory. It becomes evidence. Evidence defeats doubt. Doubt keeps many trapped in wage-only thinking. When you see proof of concept, belief strengthens. Stronger belief increases boldness. Boldness increases attempts. More attempts increase wins. Wins increase capital. Capital increases optionality. Optionality increases freedom. Freedom becomes tangible, not abstract.

Ownership begins small and often unimpressive. It might be a digital product, a micro-service, a tiny royalty, or a small resale margin. Size does not matter at the beginning — structure does. The structure is what scales. A small owned stream can be widened. A wide stream can be deepened. A deep stream can be replicated. Replication creates portfolio effects. Portfolio effects reduce risk. Reduced risk enables bigger bets. Bigger bets create breakthrough moments. Respect the small start.

Most people delay ownership because they overestimate complexity. They imagine massive capital and perfect knowledge are required. Many ownership paths start with skill and service. Skill can be learned. Service can be offered immediately. Offered service creates revenue. Revenue can be reinvested. Reinvestment builds assets. Assets create ownership layers. Layers create stability. Stability supports expansion. Expansion builds wealth.

Your first ownership dollar changes how you see problems. Problems become potential products. Friction becomes opportunity. Inefficiency becomes a design challenge. Complaints become market signals. You stop being only affected by systems and start improving them. Improvement is monetizable. Monetizable improvement attracts buyers. Buyers validate value. Validated value deserves scaling. Scaling deserves structure. Structure deserves ownership.

Ownership forces you to learn distribution. You must learn how value reaches people. Distribution skills are income multipliers. Marketing becomes service, not noise. Communication becomes a revenue tool. Positioning becomes strategic. Messaging becomes measurable. Testing becomes routine. Data becomes guidance. Guidance improves targeting. Better targeting increases conversion. Conversion increases return.

The discipline of ownership builds financial literacy quickly. You begin tracking costs and margins. You understand inputs and outputs. You measure return on effort. You analyze channels and results. This literacy compounds decision quality. Better decisions increase yield. Higher yield increases reinvestment power. Reinvestment increases scale speed. Scale speed increases advantage. Advantage increases income durability.

Ownership also builds resilience. When one stream slows, another can grow. Multiple streams reduce fragility. Fragility keeps people fearful. Reduced fear enables experimentation. Experimentation produces innovation. Innovation creates differentiation. Differentiation commands premium pricing. Premium pricing increases margin. Margin increases reinvestment capacity. Capacity increases staying power. Staying power wins long games.

Psychologically, ownership increases responsibility. Responsibility sharpens attention. Sharpened attention improves quality. Quality attracts trust. Trust attracts referrals. Referrals lower acquisition cost. Lower acquisition cost increases margin. Margin increases sustainability. Sustainability supports longevity. Longevity allows compounding.

Compounding builds millions. Responsibility is not burden — it is leverage.

Your first owned dollar also changes how you view spending. You become more selective. You evaluate purchases against asset potential. You ask whether money could be deployed instead. Deployment thinking increases capital efficiency. Efficient capital accelerates growth. Growth motivates discipline. Discipline protects reserves. Reserves create options. Options create strategic flexibility. Flexibility reduces desperation. Reduced desperation improves negotiation.

Ownership requires tolerance for uncertainty. Income may fluctuate at first. Fluctuation teaches adaptation. Adaptation builds strategy. Strategy improves predictability. Predictability stabilizes revenue. Stability enables planning. Planning enables scaling. Scaling increases throughput. Throughput increases profit. Profit funds expansion. Expansion widens opportunity.

Many avoid ownership because feedback becomes personal. When you own the outcome, results feel closer. That closeness is developmental. It speeds learning. Fast learning improves models. Better models improve decisions. Better decisions improve returns. Returns reinforce commitment. Commitment strengthens discipline. Discipline improves consistency. Consistency builds reputation. Reputation attracts demand.

Ownership turns you into a student of systems. You study workflows and automation. Automation multiplies effort. Multiplied effort increases output. Increased output increases reach. Reach increases revenue probability. Probability increases confidence. Confidence supports bolder scaling. Scaling increases asset value. Asset value increases net worth. Net worth measures ownership power.

You should pursue ownership even while employed. Employment can fund experimentation. Experimentation can birth assets. Assets can outgrow wages. Outgrown wages create transition options. Options reduce fear. Reduced fear improves execution. Execution improves results. Results justify expansion. Expansion builds independence. Independence becomes practical.

Your first ownership dollar is a seed, not a trophy. Seeds must be planted again. Reinvestment is planting. Planting creates future yield. Yield creates surplus. Surplus creates scaling capital. Scaling capital builds infrastructure. Infrastructure supports growth. Growth attracts partners. Partners increase capacity. Capacity increases speed. Speed increases advantage.

Ownership changes conversations. You speak in terms of value and systems. You ask about margins and channels. You discuss leverage and retention. This language attracts builders. Builders create networks. Networks create deal flow. Deal flow creates opportunity clusters. Clusters increase win probability. Probability increases confidence. Confidence sustains pursuit. Pursuit produces breakthroughs.

The transformation from broke to breakthrough accelerates at ownership. Control replaces dependency. Strategy replaces hope. Systems replace hustle alone. Assets replace only activity. Multiplication replaces limitation. Ownership is not optional for wealth — it is foundational. Start small but start now. Earn your first owned dollar. Then earn the next thousand the same way. Everything changes when you own the source.

6

SKILL STACKS BEAT LUCKY BREAKS EVERY TIME

Skill stacks beat lucky breaks because skills compound while luck evaporates. A lucky break may open a door, but only skill keeps it open. Too many people build their dreams on probability instead of capability. Probability is unstable and uncontrollable. Capability is trainable and expandable. When you stack skills, you build a machine that produces opportunity on demand. Each skill increases your surface area for value creation. Each added competency multiplies usefulness. Multiplying usefulness increases market demand. Market demand increases income options. Income options increase leverage.

Luck is an event, but skill is an engine. Events are temporary spikes. Engines produce continuous output. If your strategy depends on spikes, your income will be volatile. If your strategy depends on engines, your income becomes predictable. Skill engines can be upgraded. Upgrades increase efficiency. Efficiency increases output. Output increases return. Return funds further upgrades. Upgrades accelerate the cycle. That cycle is how wealth is engineered.

A single skill can earn you money, but a stack of skills

can earn you freedom. When complementary skills combine, they create uncommon value. Writing plus marketing plus analytics beats writing alone. Sales plus product knowledge plus communication beats sales alone. Technical ability plus teaching ability plus branding beats technical ability alone. The market pays premiums for integrated capability. Integration is rare because stacking takes discipline. Discipline filters competitors. Fewer competitors mean higher margins. Higher margins accelerate wealth building.

Lucky breaks are uncontrollable inputs. Skill stacks are controllable inputs. You cannot schedule luck. You can schedule practice. You cannot repeat luck on command. You can repeat drills daily. Repetition builds competence. Competence builds confidence. Confidence builds initiative. Initiative creates opportunity. Opportunity produces wins. Wins reinforce discipline. Discipline sustains stacking.

Skill stacking also protects you from industry shifts. Single-skill professionals are fragile. Multi-skill builders are adaptive. Adaptability reduces risk. Reduced risk increases longevity. Longevity increases compounding time. Compounding time multiplies results. Results build capital. Capital funds learning. Learning adds skills. Added skills increase adaptability again. The loop strengthens resilience.

Many people chase breakthroughs instead of building stacks. They look for one big moment. Big moments are unreliable. Daily reps are reliable. Small improvements accumulate quietly. Quiet accumulation creates loud outcomes. Outcomes look sudden to outsiders. Insiders know they were built slowly. Slow builds last longer. Lasting value produces recurring revenue. Recurring revenue stabilizes growth. Stability supports scale.

Skill stacks increase your problem-solving range. The

more tools you hold, the more problems you can fix. Problems are profit opportunities. Profit follows solutions. More solutions equal more income channels. Multiple channels reduce dependence. Reduced dependence increases negotiation power. Negotiation power increases earnings. Earnings fund further skill acquisition. Skill acquisition expands range again. Range increases value density.

Stacking begins with identifying a core skill. Your core skill is your base engine. Then add adjacent skills that increase its value. Adjacent skills multiply output instead of distracting focus. Focused adjacency creates synergy. Synergy produces exponential results. Exponential results beat linear effort. Linear effort caps income. Exponential capacity breaks ceilings. Ceilings are broken by combinations. Combinations are built deliberately.

Learning skills without applying them is stacking in theory only. Applied skills generate feedback. Feedback refines technique. Refined technique improves performance. Improved performance increases value. Increased value attracts buyers. Buyers validate stacks. Validated stacks deserve scaling. Scaling produces leverage. Leverage multiplies income. Income funds mastery. Mastery deepens stacks.

Skill stacking requires tolerance for being bad at new things. Early incompetence is temporary. Avoiding it creates permanent limitation. Push through awkward phases. Awkward reps build neural wiring. Neural wiring builds fluency. Fluency builds speed. Speed builds efficiency. Efficiency increases output. Output increases return. Return funds better tools. Better tools improve results.

Time allocation reveals stacking seriousness. If all your time goes to maintenance, stacking stalls. Dedicate protected hours to skill growth. Growth hours are wealth hours. Treat them as non-negotiable. Non-negotiable practice produces progress. Progress builds motivation. Motivation supports consistency. Consistency produces compounding. Compounding creates advantage. Advantage increases income velocity. Velocity accelerates breakthrough.

Skill stacks also improve creativity. Cross-domain knowledge sparks innovation. Innovation creates differentiation. Differentiation commands premium pricing. Premium pricing increases margin. Margin increases reinvestment. Reinvestment funds exploration. Exploration adds new skills. New skills create new combinations. New combinations open new markets. New markets expand reach. Reach multiplies revenue.

Mentorship accelerates stacking speed. Learning from practitioners shortens error cycles. Shorter error cycles reduce cost. Reduced cost increases iteration. Iteration improves quality. Quality increases reputation. Reputation attracts opportunity. Opportunity brings higher-level problems. Higher-level problems build higher-level skills. Higher-level skills increase earning power. Earning power funds elite training. Elite training sharpens stacks.

Skill stacks turn effort into leverage. Instead of working harder, you work more powerfully. Powerful work produces outsized results. Outsized results create strategic options. Options reduce desperation. Reduced desperation improves decisions. Better decisions increase yield. Yield increases reinvestment. Reinvestment builds assets. Assets create ownership. Ownership multiplies wealth.

Luck stories are often stacked skill stories in disguise. What looks sudden is usually prepared. Preparation meets opportunity and appears magical. Remove preparation and opportunity is wasted. Prepared people capture breaks.

Unprepared people miss them. Capture converts chance into income. Income funds further preparation. Further preparation increases capture rate. Capture rate increases success frequency. Frequency creates momentum.

Skill stacking is also a confidence strategy. Each added competency reduces fear. Reduced fear increases initiative. Initiative produces attempts. Attempts produce learning. Learning improves performance. Performance builds proof. Proof builds belief. Belief fuels ambition. Ambition drives deeper stacking. Deeper stacking builds authority.

Authority comes from demonstrated multi-skill value. Authority attracts premium opportunities. Premium opportunities pay more per effort unit. Higher pay per unit accelerates goals. Faster goals sustain motivation. Sustained motivation supports discipline. Discipline maintains stacking habits. Habits create identity. Identity shapes behavior. Behavior shapes income. Income shapes lifestyle.

Your first million is more likely to come from stacked usefulness than singular brilliance. Become dangerously useful across related domains. Useful people get hired, retained, and referred. Referrals reduce acquisition friction. Reduced friction increases deal flow. Deal flow increases wins. Wins build capital. Capital funds advanced learning. Advanced learning sharpens stacks further. Stacks create unfair advantage.

Do not wait for a lucky break — manufacture repeated readiness. Build skill layers weekly. Combine them intentionally. Apply them publicly. Measure results honestly. Improve them relentlessly. Teach them generously. Sell them confidently. Scale them systematically. Skill stacks beat lucky breaks every time because they turn you into the opportunity.

7

IF IT DOESN'T PRODUCE, IT DOESN'T BELONG IN YOUR SCHEDULE

If it doesn't produce, it doesn't belong in your schedule — that is not harsh, it is honest. Your calendar is your financial blueprint written in hours instead of dollars. Every block of time either builds capacity, creates value, or maintains survival. Only one of those creates wealth. Many people confuse motion with production. They fill days with activity but produce nothing measurable. Production means output that can be used, sold, improved, or scaled. Busy is not bankable. Output is bankable. Your schedule must become a production tool, not a comfort list.

Production is not limited to direct revenue tasks, but it must connect to revenue roots. Skill building produces future income. Asset creation produces recurring income. Relationship building with purpose produces opportunity income. System building produces leveraged income. Recovery that protects performance produces sustainable income. But distraction produces nothing. Aimless browsing produces nothing. Reactive task switching produces nothing durable. Unplanned days produce accidental results. Accidental results rarely create wealth.

Your schedule is currently telling the truth about your priorities whether you like it or not. You may say wealth matters, but your hours may disagree. Time is more honest than intention. When you audit your week, production gaps appear quickly. Gaps reveal drift. Drift destroys momentum. Momentum is required for compounding. Compounding requires consistency. Consistency requires structure. Structure requires scheduling. Scheduling requires courage to say no. No is a wealth word.

High performers schedule production first and everything else second. Creation blocks go at peak energy hours. Deep work is protected, not postponed. Notifications are silenced, not negotiated with. Focus is engineered, not hoped for. Production requires uninterrupted concentration. Concentration creates quality. Quality creates demand. Demand creates revenue. Revenue creates reinvestment. Reinvestment creates scale.

Low producers schedule comfort first and production later. Later rarely arrives. Energy declines through the day. Distractions multiply by afternoon. Decision fatigue weakens discipline. Weak discipline delays output. Delayed output kills momentum. Dead momentum kills motivation. Lost motivation fuels avoidance. Avoidance fills schedules with trivial tasks. Trivial tasks create trivial income. The pattern repeats until interrupted.

Every task should face a production question. Does this build skill, asset, system, or opportunity. If not, it is maintenance or distraction. Maintenance should be minimized and batched. Distraction should be eliminated or restricted. Production should be expanded and protected. Protection requires boundaries. Boundaries require communication. Communication requires clarity. Clarity requires decision.

Decision requires commitment. Commitment creates results.

Meetings are one of the biggest production leaks. Many meetings create conversation but no construction. Conversation without decision is waste. Decision without action is delay. Action without follow-through is decay. Every meeting should produce a next step. Every next step should have an owner. Ownership creates accountability. Accountability creates execution. Execution creates output. Output creates progress. Progress creates revenue potential.

Digital time must pass a production filter. Tools are either used to build or to consume. Building tools deserve priority. Consumption tools deserve limits. Limits protect attention. Attention fuels output. Output builds assets. Assets generate income. Income funds freedom. Freedom expands choice. Choice strengthens leverage. Leverage multiplies results.

Production scheduling also means sequencing difficulty first. Hard things produce disproportionate return. Easy things produce emotional comfort. Emotional comfort is not economic progress. Do the hardest value task first daily. Early wins create psychological momentum. Momentum reduces resistance. Reduced resistance increases throughput. Throughput increases output volume. Volume increases probability of success. Success reinforces discipline. Discipline stabilizes routine.

Metrics must be attached to production time. Measured work improves faster. Track pages written, calls made, offers sent, prototypes built. Measurement reveals truth. Truth drives adjustment. Adjustment increases efficiency. Efficiency increases yield. Yield increases motivation. Motivation sustains consistency. Consistency builds compounding output. Compounding output builds wealth.

Production blocks should be distraction-proof by design. Environment shapes behavior more than willpower. Remove friction to start. Add friction to distractions. Pre-stage tools for work. Hide tools for drift. Design supports discipline. Discipline supports output. Output supports income. Income supports reinvestment. Reinvestment supports scale. Scale supports wealth.

Your schedule should reflect value hierarchy. High-value tasks get prime placement. Low-value tasks get leftovers or elimination. Many people reverse this. They spend their best hours on low stakes. They give their tired hours to high stakes. That mismatch produces weak results. Align energy with importance. Importance determines return. Return determines growth speed. Growth speed determines breakthrough timing. Timing matters financially.

Production also includes thinking time with intent. Strategic thinking is productive when directed. Undirected worry is not. Plan systems, offers, and improvements. Design experiments and tests. Thinking that leads to action is production. Thinking that replaces action is delay. Delay is expensive. Directed thought creates leverage. Leverage multiplies output. Output multiplies income. Income multiplies options.

Rest must be scheduled as performance support, not escape. Recovery protects production capacity. Exhaustion reduces output quality. Low quality reduces market value. Reduced value reduces income. Proper rest increases clarity. Clarity improves decisions. Better decisions increase yield. Yield increases motivation. Motivation supports discipline. Discipline protects production blocks.

If a recurring task produces nothing, redesign or remove it. Automation can replace repetition. Delegation can replace overload. Elimination can replace tradition. Tradition without production is nostalgia. Nostalgia is not a revenue model. Models must produce measurable value. Measurable value deserves time. Time investment should show return. Return validates scheduling. Validation builds confidence.

Production culture must extend to your environment and peers. Surround yourself with builders. Builders normalize output. Output becomes expected. Expectation raises standards. Higher standards improve performance. Improved performance increases results. Results reinforce culture. Culture sustains discipline. Discipline sustains production. Production sustains wealth building.

Saying yes to everything is saying no to production. Overcommitment fractures focus. Fractured focus weakens output. Weak output reduces results. Reduced results increase stress. Stress invites distraction. Distraction kills production blocks. Protect your yes carefully. Guard your calendar aggressively. Time is capital. Capital must be invested wisely. Wise investment creates growth.

Your first million will not come from a full calendar — it will come from a productive one. Full is not fruitful. Busy is not bankable. Only producing time multiplies money. Build days around creation. Build weeks around delivery. Build months around assets. Build years around systems. Systems scale beyond you. Scale creates breakthrough. Breakthrough follows production discipline.

8

SPEED BEATS PERFECTION — MOVE BEFORE YOU FEEL READY

Perfection is a beautiful excuse that quietly murders momentum. It sounds noble, disciplined, and high-standard, but in practice it delays more wealth than laziness ever does. Speed, on the other hand, feels reckless to the cautious mind but is often the true ally of progress. The marketplace rewards finished and functional far more than flawless and fictional. An imperfect offer in motion can earn, learn, and improve. A perfect plan in your head earns nothing and teaches nothing. Movement generates feedback faster than contemplation. Feedback generates correction faster than theory. Correction generates competence faster than caution. If you wait to feel ready, you will wait past your opportunity window.

Readiness is rarely a feeling — it is a decision followed by motion. Most people expect confidence before action, but confidence is usually the result of action. The first step feels unstable because it is new, not because it is wrong. Instability is a training signal, not a stop sign. Early discomfort is tuition, not tragedy. Tuition paid through action buys experience. Experience produces judgment. Judgment improves decisions. Better decisions increase return. Return builds confidence. Confidence then fuels faster movement.

Speed is not sloppiness — it is decisiveness with iteration. Moving fast does not mean ignoring quality; it means reaching quality through cycles instead of delays. Version one teaches what version ten in your head never will. Real users expose real flaws. Real flaws create real fixes. Real fixes produce real improvement. Improvement compounds through repetition. Repetition builds mastery. Mastery increases efficiency. Efficiency increases output. Output increases income probability.

Perfectionists overprotect reputation and underproduce results. They polish invisible work instead of shipping visible value. Visible value can be evaluated. Evaluation produces data. Data produces direction. Direction accelerates progress. Hidden work produces none of this. Hidden work earns no feedback. No feedback means no refinement. No refinement means no growth. No growth means no scale. No scale means no breakthrough.

Speed expands your opportunity surface area. More attempts create more chances for wins. More wins create more capital. More capital creates more reinvestment. More reinvestment creates more scale. Scale increases reach. Reach increases deal flow. Deal flow increases conversion probability. Probability favors volume of quality attempts. Volume requires speed. Speed requires courage to release early.

The fear behind perfection is usually fear of judgment. Judgment feels personal but is often informational. Market response is data, not identity. Separate your worth from your work. Work can improve rapidly. Worth is not on trial. When you detach ego from output, speed increases. Increased speed accelerates learning loops. Faster learning loops produce sharper strategy. Sharper strategy improves results. Results reinforce bold execution.

Momentum is a financial asset. Slow starters rarely build large momentum. Quick movers build early traction. Traction attracts attention. Attention attracts opportunity. Opportunity attracts partnership. Partnership expands capacity. Capacity increases output. Output increases revenue potential. Potential turns into profit through repetition. Momentum reduces friction each step forward.

Perfection delays revenue while expenses continue. Speed shortens the distance to first cash flow. First cash flow funds improvement. Improvement increases quality. Quality increases retention. Retention increases lifetime value. Lifetime value increases margin. Margin increases reinvestment ability. Reinvestment increases speed again. Speed becomes self-reinforcing. Delay becomes self-defeating.

Fast execution reveals hidden obstacles early. Early obstacles are cheaper to fix. Late obstacles are expensive to reverse. Early testing prevents large-scale failure. Small failures teach precise lessons. Precise lessons guide upgrades. Upgrades improve performance. Performance increases competitiveness. Competitiveness increases win rate. Win rate increases income stability. Stability supports scaling.

You must train decision speed deliberately. Set shorter deadlines for releases. Limit planning windows. Force shipment dates. Dates create urgency. Urgency triggers focus. Focus increases output. Output produces feedback. Feedback drives refinement. Refinement improves quality. Quality rises through cycles, not delays.

Speed also protects you from overthinking traps. Overthinking magnifies risk perception. Magnified risk perception reduces action. Reduced action kills momentum. Momentum loss increases fear. Fear increases delay. Delay increases doubt. Doubt reinforces hesitation. Hesitation blocks opportunity capture. Opportunity capture requires motion. Motion defeats mental fog.

Early movers learn market language faster. They hear customer objections directly. Direct objections reveal positioning gaps. Gaps can be fixed quickly. Quick fixes increase conversion. Conversion increases revenue. Revenue funds experimentation. Experimentation discovers advantage. Advantage improves differentiation. Differentiation commands premium pricing. Premium pricing accelerates wealth.

Perfection focuses on internal standards only. Speed integrates external response. External response is reality. Reality-guided iteration beats imagination-guided delay. Reality gives clearer signals. Clearer signals guide smarter pivots. Smarter pivots save time. Saved time increases throughput. Throughput increases attempts. Attempts increase wins. Wins increase confidence and capital.

Moving before you feel ready builds courage capacity. Courage grows through exposure. Exposure reduces fear sensitivity. Reduced fear increases initiative. Initiative produces opportunities. Opportunities produce results. Results produce proof. Proof strengthens identity. Identity shifts toward builder and executor. Builders move early. Executors ship often.

Your competitors are delayed by doubt more than defeated by difficulty. If you move while they hesitate, you gain ground. Ground gained early compounds. Compounding lead creates dominance. Dominance attracts trust. Trust attracts buyers. Buyers create revenue. Revenue creates reinvestment power. Reinvestment builds infrastructure. Infrastructure increases speed further. Speed becomes strategic advantage.

Iteration speed beats initial brilliance. Many average ideas executed quickly outperform brilliant ideas delayed endlessly. Execution exposes truth. Truth refines direction. Direction focuses effort. Focused effort increases efficiency. Efficiency increases output. Output increases results. Results justify continuation. Continuation builds mastery. Mastery increases earning power.

Set a bias toward action in your rules. When uncertain, test instead of theorize. When hesitant, ship small. When afraid, launch limited. Small launches reduce risk. Reduced risk increases speed. Increased speed increases learning. Learning increases precision. Precision improves results. Results fuel confidence to scale.

Your first million will not be built by the most careful planner. It will be built by the most disciplined executor. Execute early. Execute often. Execute imperfectly. Improve continuously. Measure honestly. Adjust quickly. Repeat relentlessly. Speed beats perfection because progress beats intention. Move before you feel ready and let readiness catch up.

9

CASH FLOW FIRST — EGO LATER

Cash flow is oxygen for your financial life, and ego is often the silent suffocator. Many people try to look successful before they become solvent. They chase image before income and status before stability. That reversal creates fragile finances wrapped in impressive appearances. Cash flow pays the bills, funds experiments, and buys time to improve. Ego buys applause that cannot cover expenses. Applause does not compound, but cash flow does. When you put ego first, you choose optics over economics. When you put cash flow first, you choose function over fantasy. Wealth is built on inflow, not impression.

Early-stage builders must become brutally cash-flow focused. Predictable money coming in beats glamorous plans going nowhere. A simple offer that sells beats a complex idea that doesn't. Revenue validates reality. Validation directs effort. Directed effort improves efficiency. Efficiency increases margin. Margin increases reinvestment power. Reinvestment accelerates growth. Growth builds optionality. Optionality builds freedom.

Ego resists small starts because small looks unimpressive. Cash flow rewards small starts because small can ship fast. Your first profitable version should be simple and useful. Usefulness converts faster than sophistication. Fast conversion produces early revenue. Early revenue funds upgrades. Upgrades improve quality. Improved quality increases retention. Retention increases lifetime value. Lifetime value increases stability. Stability enables scale.

Many delay monetization to protect identity. They want the brand perfect before the bank account functional. That is ego disguised as strategy. The market pays for value delivered, not logos perfected. Deliver first, decorate later. Function before form is a wealth principle. Form can be improved with funded iteration. Unfunded perfection is expensive delay. Funded imperfection is productive motion. Motion builds momentum. Momentum builds results.

Cash flow clarity forces honest math. Math removes emotional illusion. You see what works and what doesn't quickly. Quick truth enables fast adjustment. Fast adjustment prevents long losses. Prevented losses protect capital. Protected capital extends runway. Runway allows learning. Learning improves offers. Improved offers increase revenue velocity. Velocity accelerates breakthrough.

Ego often pushes people toward complexity. Complexity looks impressive but slows execution. Simple revenue systems scale better than complex fragile ones. Simple offers are easier to explain. Easy explanation increases conversion. Higher conversion increases cash flow. Cash flow funds complexity later if needed. Earn the right to complicate. Start with clarity and speed. Speed produces income. Income produces options.

Pricing is another battlefield between ego and cash flow. Ego prices for prestige. Cash flow prices for conversion and margin. Prestige pricing without proof kills early revenue.

Conversion pricing with value builds volume and testimonials. Testimonials build authority. Authority justifies premium later. Later premium multiplies revenue. Revenue multiplies reinvestment. Reinvestment builds infrastructure. Infrastructure supports scale.

Ego spends to be seen; cash flow spends to be sustained. Flashy expenses feel validating but drain reserves. Reserves are strategic power. Strategic power funds opportunity moves. Opportunity moves create growth. Growth creates credibility. Credibility attracts better deals. Better deals increase margin. Margin increases resilience. Resilience protects momentum. Momentum builds wealth.

Vanity metrics feed ego but starve cash flow. Followers without buyers create illusion. Traffic without conversion creates noise. Attention without revenue creates distraction. Measure money metrics first. Track revenue, margin, retention, and acquisition cost. These numbers guide decisions. Decisions guided by numbers improve yield. Improved yield increases profit. Profit funds expansion. Expansion builds scale.

Cash flow focus changes how you design work. You ask how quickly value can reach buyers. You remove unnecessary steps. Fewer steps increase speed. Speed increases release frequency. Frequency increases testing volume. Testing volume increases learning speed. Learning speed improves positioning. Better positioning increases conversion. Conversion increases revenue. Revenue builds confidence and capital.

Ego hates unglamorous revenue streams. Maintenance contracts, small services, and repeatable gigs look boring. Boring money is often stable money. Stable money funds bold experiments. Experiments produce innovation. Innovation creates breakthroughs. Breakthroughs look glamorous later. Later glory is funded by early grind. Grind produces cash flow. Cash flow produces staying power. Staying power wins markets.

Partnership decisions must also pass the cash flow filter. Some partnerships boost image but reduce margin. Others boost margin but stay quiet publicly. Choose margin early. Margin gives you independence. Independence gives you negotiation leverage. Leverage improves deal terms. Better terms increase profit. Profit increases reinvestment. Reinvestment increases ownership. Ownership builds net worth. Net worth builds freedom.

Cash flow discipline requires saying no to ego projects. Not every exciting idea deserves immediate pursuit. Sequence matters. Fund the engine first. Then build the extras. Extras without engine stall. Engine without extras still runs. Running businesses can be optimized. Stalled businesses cannot be saved by style. Style follows substance. Substance is funded by revenue. Revenue is fueled by value delivered.

Your calendar should reflect cash flow priority. Revenue-producing tasks get prime hours. Support tasks get secondary hours. Ego tasks get leftovers or deletion. This ordering creates financial gravity. Gravity pulls results forward. Forward motion increases momentum. Momentum increases confidence. Confidence increases assertive action. Assertive action increases deal flow. Deal flow increases revenue probability.

Cash flow also reduces emotional volatility. Money coming in stabilizes decision-making. Stability improves judgment. Better judgment improves allocation. Allocation improves return on effort. Higher return accelerates growth. Growth reduces desperation. Reduced desperation improves negotiation. Better negotiation increases margin. Margin increases reserves. Reserves increase confidence.

Ego wants immediate scale; cash flow builds gradual scale. Gradual scale is durable scale. Durable scale survives stress. Stress tests every business. Cash-flow-strong models pass more tests. Passing tests builds reputation. Reputation attracts repeat buyers. Repeat buyers lower acquisition cost. Lower acquisition cost increases profit. Profit funds automation. Automation increases leverage.

Marketing should be judged by cash results, not creativity awards. Creative that converts beats creative that impresses. Conversion funds campaigns. Funded campaigns increase reach. Increased reach increases revenue chances. Revenue chances justify experimentation. Experimentation improves messaging. Messaging improves conversion again. The loop strengthens through money metrics. Measure what pays.

Ego later does not mean ego never. It means ego is sequenced after sustainability. Once cash flow is strong, brand elevation is strategic. Strategic brand building multiplies trust. Trust multiplies conversion. Conversion multiplies revenue. Revenue multiplies options. Options multiply impact. Impact multiplies legacy. Legacy is funded by earlier discipline. Discipline chooses cash flow first.

Your first million is built on financial oxygen, not public admiration. Breathe through revenue. Build through margin. Grow through reinvestment. Scale through systems. Polish later. Impress later. Expand later. But earn now. Cash flow first — ego later — always.

10

TURN ONE OFFER INTO TEN INCOME STREAMS

Turning one offer into ten income streams is not duplication — it is intelligent expansion. Most people create once and sell once, then start over from zero. Builders create once and extract value repeatedly. The difference is leverage thinking. Your first offer is not just a product — it is a platform. Inside every good offer are multiple deliverables waiting to be separated, repackaged, and redistributed. One solution can serve different segments in different formats. Format variation multiplies reach. Reach multiplies revenue paths. Revenue paths multiply stability. Stability multiplies confidence to scale.

The first mistake amateurs make is abandoning a working offer too early. They get bored before the market gets saturated. Master builders stay longer and dig deeper. Depth reveals hidden assets inside the original work. A core offer contains frameworks, steps, tools, stories, and systems. Each component can become its own micro-offer. Micro-offers attract niche buyers. Niche buyers convert at higher rates. Higher conversion increases total yield. Yield funds further expansion. Expansion multiplies streams.

Start by breaking your core offer into layers. There is a beginner layer, an intermediate layer, and an advanced layer. Each layer can be sold separately. Separation increases accessibility. Accessibility increases buyer count. More buyers increase data. Data reveals demand pockets. Demand pockets guide new variations. Variations create new revenue channels. Channels reduce dependence on one stream. Reduced dependence increases resilience. Resilience supports growth.

Next, multiply formats aggressively. One offer can become a book, a workbook, a course, a workshop, and a consulting package. It can become a checklist, a template set, and a video series. It can become a live cohort and a recorded library. It can become a certification track. Format shifts reach different learning preferences. Different preferences unlock different buyers. Different buyers create diversified income. Diversified income stabilizes cash flow. Stability supports reinvestment. Reinvestment accelerates scaling.

Price tiers create vertical streams from the same core value. Entry-level versions lower the barrier. Mid-tier versions increase depth. Premium versions increase access and customization. Tiering captures multiple budgets. Multiple budgets expand total market capture. Capture increases revenue density. Revenue density improves margin. Margin funds marketing. Marketing increases reach. Reach feeds tiers. Tiers multiply streams.

Licensing is another powerful stream multiplier. Instead of selling only to end users, sell usage rights to other providers. Providers distribute to their audiences. Audience borrowing accelerates scale. Scale increases royalty flow. Royalty flow becomes recurring revenue. Recurring revenue stabilizes planning. Planning enables long-term investment.

Investment improves infrastructure. Infrastructure supports volume. Volume multiplies income.

Bundle strategy multiplies perceived value. Combine your core offer with complementary tools. Bundles raise average order value. Higher order value increases revenue per buyer. Revenue per buyer improves acquisition economics. Better acquisition economics justify paid traffic. Paid traffic increases scale speed. Scale speed increases total revenue. Total revenue funds new bundle creation. New bundles attract new segments. Segments create new streams.

Subscription models convert one-time offers into recurring streams. Recurring access creates predictable revenue. Predictability improves cash flow planning. Planning supports hiring and automation. Automation increases delivery efficiency. Efficiency increases margin. Margin increases reinvestment capacity. Reinvestment expands content and tools. Expanded resources increase retention. Retention increases lifetime value. Lifetime value multiplies income per customer.

Consulting and services can spin off from a core offer. Some buyers want implementation help. Implementation help commands premium pricing. Premium pricing increases revenue concentration. Concentrated revenue funds product refinement. Refinement improves outcomes. Improved outcomes create testimonials. Testimonials increase trust. Trust increases conversion. Conversion increases demand for services. Services create another stream.

Affiliate and partner versions create distribution streams. Let others sell your offer for a share. Shared revenue expands reach faster. Faster reach increases volume. Volume increases brand presence. Presence builds authority. Authority improves conversion. Conversion increases affiliate interest. More affiliates increase distribution. Distribution increases total income. Income multiplies with minimal added effort.

Content atomization creates micro-streams. Break your offer into short guides, cheat sheets, and mini-trainings. Micro-assets sell at impulse price points. Impulse pricing increases conversion frequency. Frequency increases total transactions. Transactions increase revenue flow. Flow improves cash stability. Stability supports experimentation. Experimentation produces new micro-assets. New assets expand catalogs. Catalogs multiply streams.

Events and experiences are another expansion path. Host workshops and intensives based on your core offer. Live events command premium pricing. Premium pricing increases revenue spikes. Revenue spikes fund development. Development improves core material. Improved material increases satisfaction. Satisfaction drives referrals. Referrals increase attendance. Attendance multiplies event income. Events become repeatable streams.

Certification programs convert knowledge into credentials. Credentials attract career-driven buyers. Career buyers invest more. Higher investment increases revenue per seat. Revenue per seat supports support staff. Support staff improves delivery. Better delivery increases outcomes. Outcomes increase program prestige. Prestige increases demand. Demand increases pricing power. Pricing power increases margin.

Community access can be monetized as a stream. Build a network around your offer. Networks create peer value. Peer value increases stickiness. Stickiness reduces churn. Reduced churn increases recurring revenue. Recurring revenue stabilizes growth. Growth funds community tools.

Better tools increase engagement. Engagement increases retention. Retention multiplies lifetime value.

Data gathered from your first offer is itself an asset. Insights reveal unmet needs. Unmet needs guide new offers. New offers extend the ecosystem. Ecosystems create cross-sell streams. Cross-sells increase revenue per buyer. Higher revenue per buyer improves acquisition ROI. Better ROI enables scale. Scale increases data again. Data refines targeting. Targeting increases conversion.

Language and localization can multiply streams globally. Translate your offer. New languages open new markets. New markets add new buyers. Buyers add new revenue flow. Flow justifies localized marketing. Local marketing increases penetration. Penetration increases brand reach. Reach multiplies influence. Influence attracts partnerships. Partnerships add streams.

Technology layers can be added onto core offers. Turn frameworks into software tools. Tools create subscription revenue. Subscription revenue increases predictability. Predictability supports valuation growth. Higher valuation increases opportunity. Opportunity attracts investors or buyers. Buyers create exit options. Exit options create wealth events. Wealth events fund new ventures. New ventures reuse the core offer model.

The rule is simple but powerful: never create value once when you can deploy it ten ways. Extract every usable component. Repackage every functional piece. Redistribute every helpful insight. Systematize expansion deliberately. Build an offer ecosystem, not a single product. Ecosystems produce compounding streams. Compounding streams produce financial momentum. Momentum produces breakthrough. Your first million is rarely one stream — it is one offer multiplied relentlessly.

11

RELENTLESS EXECUTION: THE MILLIONAIRE'S REAL SUPERPOWER

Relentless execution is the real superpower behind nearly every self-made millionaire story. Not genius, not luck, not perfect timing — execution. Ideas are common, but completed actions are rare. Plans are everywhere, but shipped results are scarce. The marketplace does not reward what you intend — it rewards what you finish. Execution turns imagination into inventory. Execution turns strategy into sales. Execution turns goals into cash flow. Without execution, intelligence is unused horsepower. With execution, even average ideas can produce extraordinary outcomes.

Relentless execution means you produce on days you feel inspired and on days you feel flat. Motivation becomes optional when discipline becomes installed. Waiting to feel ready slows output. Acting on commitment maintains output. Output consistency builds momentum. Momentum reduces friction. Reduced friction increases speed. Increased speed multiplies attempts. More attempts increase wins. Wins build capital. Capital funds scale.

Execution is measurable while intention is not. You

cannot deposit intention. You cannot invoice intention. You cannot scale intention. But you can track calls made, offers sent, pages built, and products shipped. Measurement drives accountability. Accountability drives behavior. Behavior drives results. Results drive revenue. Revenue drives reinvestment. Reinvestment drives expansion. Expansion drives wealth.

Relentless executors remove negotiation with trivial resistance. They start before comfort appears. They begin before clarity is perfect. They move while uncertainty exists. Movement creates clarity faster than waiting. Clarity accelerates direction. Direction improves efficiency. Efficiency increases output. Output increases opportunity. Opportunity increases income probability. Probability improves through repetition.

Procrastination is not laziness — it is mismanaged emotion. Execution cuts through emotional fog with action. Action creates traction. Traction builds confidence. Confidence reduces hesitation. Reduced hesitation increases pace. Pace increases volume. Volume increases learning. Learning increases precision. Precision increases conversion. Conversion increases revenue.

Execution requires decision speed. Slow decisions create backlog. Backlog creates stress. Stress reduces performance. Fast decisions keep flow moving. Flow maintains momentum. Momentum sustains motivation. Motivation fuels continued action. Continued action produces cumulative results. Cumulative results create advantage. Advantage increases income velocity.

Relentless execution is structured, not chaotic. It uses systems and checklists. Systems reduce cognitive load. Reduced load increases consistency. Consistency increases output reliability. Reliable output builds trust. Trust attracts buyers. Buyers create revenue. Revenue funds system upgrades. Upgrades increase throughput. Throughput increases scale.

Perfectionists hesitate; executors iterate. Iteration beats hesitation financially. Each iteration improves product-market fit. Better fit increases conversion. Conversion increases revenue speed. Speed increases compounding rate. Compounding produces disproportionate outcomes. Outcomes justify persistence. Persistence builds mastery. Mastery improves execution quality. Quality attracts premium pricing.

Execution also means finishing what you start. Half-built projects produce zero return. Finished projects produce data and revenue. Finish lines create feedback. Feedback creates improvement. Improvement increases effectiveness. Effectiveness increases yield. Yield increases motivation. Motivation supports more finishing. More finishing multiplies assets. Assets multiply streams.

Relentless executors build daily output quotas. Quotas create clarity. Clarity removes ambiguity. Removed ambiguity increases start speed. Faster starts increase total production. Production builds inventory. Inventory creates selling opportunities. Selling opportunities create revenue. Revenue creates reinvestment fuel. Fuel supports scaling. Scaling increases wealth probability.

Excuse elimination is part of execution culture. Reasons are examined, not obeyed. Constraints are engineered around. Engineering creates alternatives. Alternatives enable continuation. Continuation preserves momentum. Momentum compounds effort. Compounded effort multiplies results. Results weaken future excuses. Weak excuses lose power. Power shifts to discipline.

Environment design supports relentless action. Tools are

prepared in advance. Distractions are removed proactively. Prepared spaces reduce startup friction. Reduced friction increases execution frequency. Frequency builds rhythm. Rhythm stabilizes behavior. Stable behavior produces predictable output. Predictable output builds reliability. Reliability builds reputation. Reputation attracts opportunity.

Execution energy is protected fiercely. Sleep, movement, and nutrition are treated as performance assets. High energy increases work quality. Quality increases conversion. Conversion increases revenue. Revenue reduces stress. Reduced stress preserves energy. Energy sustains execution. Sustained execution builds compounding output. Output builds wealth. Health supports long-term dominance.

Relentless execution ignores emotional weather. Bad moods do not cancel production. Good moods do not replace discipline. Discipline is weatherproof. Weatherproof habits produce steady output. Steady output compounds. Compounding output beats sporadic brilliance. Brilliance without repetition is fragile. Repetition without brilliance is powerful. Power creates results. Results create leverage.

Executors create feedback loops quickly. Fast feedback improves strategy. Improved strategy increases hit rate. Higher hit rate increases revenue efficiency. Efficiency reduces waste. Reduced waste increases margin. Margin increases reinvestment. Reinvestment increases capability. Capability improves execution again. Execution strength compounds. Compounding creates breakthroughs.

Relentless execution includes follow-up. Most deals close in follow-up, not first contact. Follow-up multiplies conversion. Conversion multiplies revenue. Revenue multiplies reinvestment capacity. Capacity funds outreach scale. Scale increases opportunity count. Opportunity count increases wins. Wins reinforce follow-up discipline. Discipline sustains pipeline flow. Flow stabilizes income.

Time blocking protects execution windows. Protected windows produce deep work. Deep work creates high-value output. High-value output attracts premium buyers. Premium buyers increase revenue per deal. Higher revenue per deal accelerates goals. Faster goals sustain motivation. Sustained motivation reinforces discipline. Discipline protects time blocks. Time blocks protect execution.

Relentless executors track lagging and leading indicators. Leading indicators show activity. Lagging indicators show results. Activity drives results eventually. Tracking activity maintains pressure. Pressure maintains output. Output produces revenue later. Later revenue validates present discipline. Validation strengthens habit. Habit becomes identity. Identity becomes unstoppable executor.

The millionaire edge is not secret knowledge — it is sustained action. Do the work daily. Ship the work weekly. Improve the work monthly. Scale the work yearly. Repeat without drama. Repeat without excuse. Repeat without waiting for applause. Execution is the compounding force. Relentless execution is the millionaire's real superpower.

12

NO FINISH LINE — ONLY FINANCIAL EXPANSION

There is no finish line in wealth building — only expanding horizons and rising capacity. The idea that you "arrive" financially is comforting but misleading. Every level of income creates a new level of responsibility and opportunity. If you treat a milestone like a destination, you will stall at it. If you treat it like a platform, you will launch from it. Expansion thinking keeps you adaptive, alert, and ambitious. It prevents complacency after early wins. Early wins are foundations, not finales. The first million is not the end goal — it is proof of process. Process is what scales beyond milestones.

A finish-line mindset creates maintenance behavior. Expansion mindset creates multiplication behavior. Maintenance protects what exists. Multiplication grows what exists. Protection alone does not build wealth velocity. Growth does. Velocity matters because time is finite. Faster intelligent growth increases lifetime opportunity capture. Opportunity capture increases total return. Total return increases strategic freedom. Freedom enables bolder expansion. Bold expansion multiplies outcomes.

Financial expansion is not only about earning more — it is about becoming more capable. Capability expansion precedes income expansion. You grow your skills, judgment, network, and systems. Each layer of growth increases your earning bandwidth. Bandwidth determines how much opportunity you can handle. Increased bandwidth supports larger deals. Larger deals produce larger returns. Larger returns fund deeper infrastructure. Infrastructure supports scale. Scale accelerates expansion.

People who stop at targets become fragile. Markets change and skills age. Expansion builders keep upgrading. Upgrading prevents obsolescence. Relevance preserves income streams. Preserved streams support reinvestment. Reinvestment funds innovation. Innovation opens new markets. New markets create new streams. New streams reduce risk. Reduced risk enables bolder moves. Motion continues.

Expansion requires reinvestment discipline. Extracting all profits slows growth. Reinvesting a portion accelerates it. Capital redeployed multiplies capacity. Capacity multiplies output. Output multiplies revenue. Revenue multiplies options. Options multiply resilience. Resilience protects progress. Protected progress sustains expansion cycles. Cycles compound wealth. Compounding beats static saving.

No finish line also means continuous optimization. Systems can always improve. Offers can always convert better. Processes can always speed up. Speed increases throughput. Throughput increases yield. Yield increases margin. Margin increases reinvestment. Reinvestment improves systems again. Improvement loops create compounding advantage. Advantage expands market share.

Expansion thinkers measure ceilings and raise them deliberately. They ask what constraint limits growth now.

Constraint removal unlocks next level output. Next level output changes economics. Changed economics enable bigger plays. Bigger plays create asymmetric upside. Upside funds diversification. Diversification stabilizes expansion. Stability supports risk-taking. Risk-taking fuels growth. Growth continues.

Your identity must expand with your income. Old self-concepts create new income ceilings. Upgrade how you see your role. Become allocator, builder, investor, owner. Each identity layer changes decisions. Decisions change outcomes. Outcomes change capacity. Capacity changes opportunity scale. Scale changes strategy. Strategy changes results. Results reinforce identity.

Expansion also applies to network quality. Higher-level rooms expose bigger problems. Bigger problems pay better. Better pay funds stronger teams. Stronger teams increase output capacity. Capacity increases deal size tolerance. Larger deals create larger returns. Returns attract elite partners. Elite partners increase reach. Reach multiplies opportunity. Opportunity multiplies expansion speed.

Geographic and market expansion multiply streams. New regions add new buyers. New buyers add new revenue. Revenue diversification reduces volatility. Reduced volatility supports bold investment. Bold investment accelerates scaling. Scaling increases brand gravity. Brand gravity attracts inbound opportunity. Inbound opportunity lowers acquisition cost. Lower cost increases margin. Margin funds further expansion.

Expansion requires curiosity discipline. Stay a student while you lead. Learning reveals emerging trends. Trends reveal early opportunities. Early opportunities pay premiums. Premium returns fund research. Research guides positioning. Positioning improves capture rate. Capture rate increases win frequency. Win frequency builds momentum. Momentum sustains expansion energy.

Complacency is the enemy of expansion. Comfort after success breeds stagnation. Stagnation invites disruption by others. Others moving faster take market share. Lost share reduces growth. Reduced growth weakens resilience. Weak resilience increases risk. Stay constructively dissatisfied. Dissatisfaction fuels improvement. Improvement fuels expansion. Expansion protects dominance.

Financial expansion also includes asset class diversity. Move beyond single income types. Add equity, intellectual property, and automation. Each asset class behaves differently. Different behavior smooths volatility. Smooth volatility improves planning. Planning improves allocation. Allocation improves return. Return funds new asset classes. Portfolio expansion multiplies stability. Stability supports ambition.

Expansion is easier with documented processes. Documentation enables delegation. Delegation increases capacity. Capacity supports more projects. More projects create more streams. Streams diversify income. Diversified income stabilizes growth. Stability supports scaling. Scaling multiplies reach. Reach increases deal flow. Deal flow fuels expansion.

Tax strategy and structure expansion matter too. Better structures preserve profit. Preserved profit increases reinvestment pool. Larger pools fund bigger moves. Bigger moves create bigger returns. Returns justify expert advisors. Advisors improve strategy. Strategy improves efficiency. Efficiency increases net yield. Net yield accelerates compounding. Compounding expands wealth.

Technology adoption accelerates expansion curves. Automation reduces manual drag. Reduced drag increases throughput. Throughput increases revenue speed. Revenue speed improves cash cycles. Faster cycles enable quicker reinvestment. Quick reinvestment captures momentum. Momentum amplifies scale. Scale strengthens market position. Position supports premium pricing. Premium pricing multiplies returns.

Expansion includes impact and influence growth. Teaching others multiplies reach. Reach multiplies opportunity flow. Opportunity flow multiplies deals. Deals multiply income. Income multiplies investment power. Investment power multiplies asset ownership. Ownership multiplies net worth. Net worth multiplies strategic options. Options multiply expansion paths. Paths stay open.

There is no finish line — only better questions. What can scale next. What can automate next. What can multiply next. What can be removed next. What can be improved next. Questions drive innovation. Innovation drives growth. Growth drives expansion. Expansion drives wealth. Keep moving outward.

Your first million is not the summit — it is base camp. From there, visibility increases. Options increase. Responsibility increases. So must your vision. Stay building. Stay reinvesting. Stay upgrading. Stay expanding. No finish line — only financial expansion.

AFTERWORD

This is where the excuses officially expire. Not tomorrow. Not next quarter. Not when conditions are cleaner and confidence feels higher. Right here is the line between intention and execution, between drifting and building, between wishing and winning. You now know the truth most people avoid — wealth is not a mystery reserved for the gifted, the lucky, or the connected. It is built by those who decide, act, adjust, and continue. The path is practical, but it is not painless. It will demand discipline when you feel distracted, courage when you feel uncertain, and persistence when you feel slow. Good — that is the price of transformation.

Your first million is not just a number — it is a new identity forged through repeated proof that you finish what you start. You are no longer waiting for permission. You are no longer negotiating with comfort. You are no longer hiding behind preparation. You are building skill stacks, protecting production time, prioritizing cash flow, multiplying offers, and executing relentlessly. You are moving before you feel ready and learning faster than you fail. That is how breakthroughs actually happen — not in one leap, but in thousands of disciplined steps.

Some will watch. Some will doubt. Some will delay their own start and try to explain why yours won't work. Let them talk while you build. Let them scroll while you construct. Let them hesitate while you execute. The market does not reward spectators — it rewards producers.

Start now. Ship something. Sell something. Improve something. Repeat daily. Your breakthrough is not coming — it is built. And it is built by you.

ALSO BY DESHAWN PRICE

Toxic Amnesia: When Survival Becomes Self-Destruction

Toxic Strength: When Survival Looks Strong but Feels Empty

Toxic Control: When Fear Disguises Itself as Safety

Toxic Validation: When Approval Replaces Identity

Toxic Loyalty: When Faithfulness Becomes Self-Betrayal

Toxic Forgiveness -: When Grace Is Given Without Boundaries

Toxic Hope: When Waiting Turns Into Wasting Away

The Monetized Viral Machine: How to Build Posts That Pay

The Story-Selling Blueprint: Influence Hearts, Not Just Feeds

Victory Protocol: Strategic Habits That Produce Daily Wins

www.ingramcontent.com/pod-product-compliance
Lightning Source LLC
LaVergne TN
LVHW090428210926
848480LV00002B/733
9798233844621